LETTER TRACING

How to write UPPERCASE letters

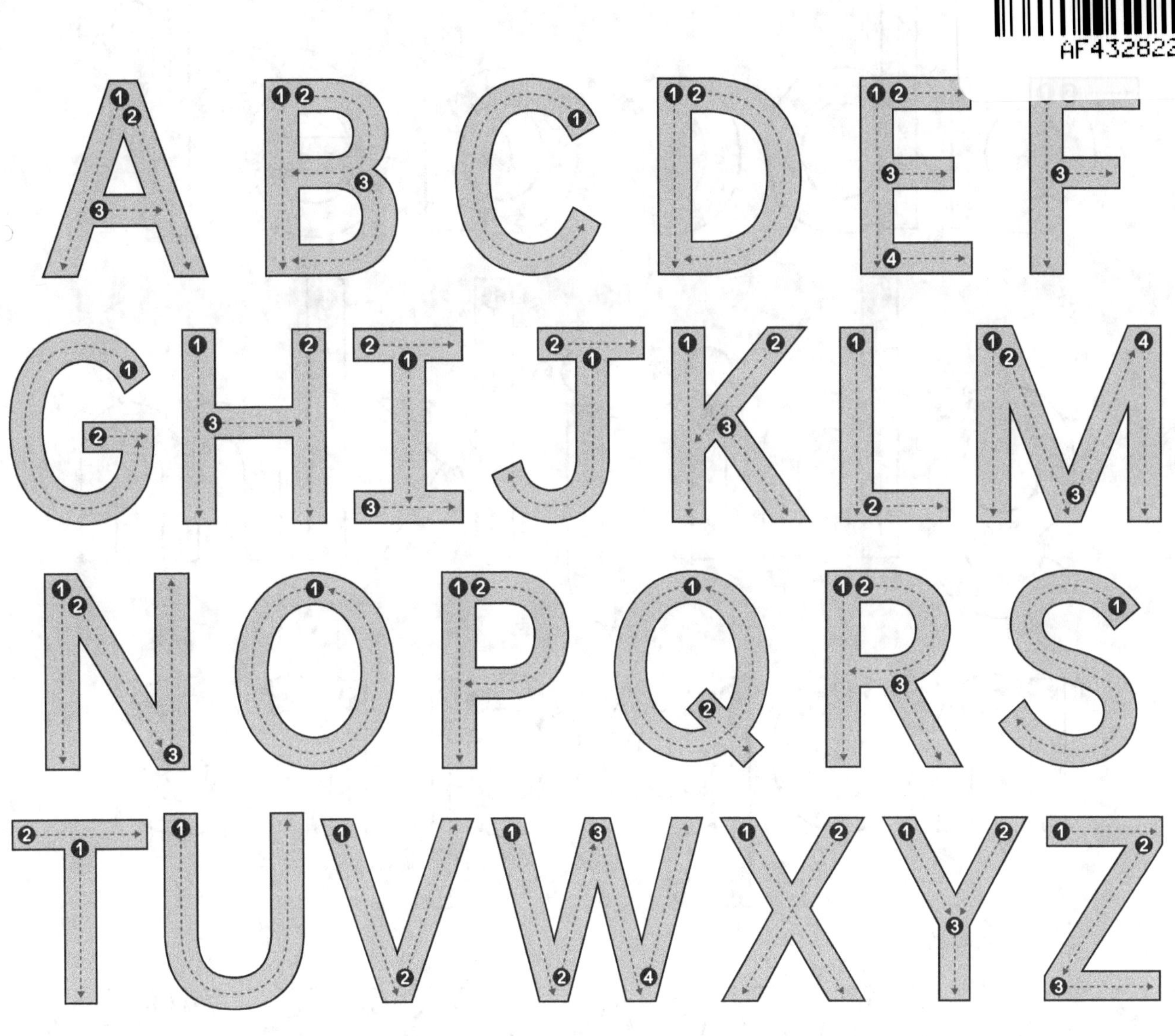

LETTER TRACING

How to write lowercase letters

A

Apple

Arrow

Ant

Acorn

A

a

apple

arrow

ant

acorn

a

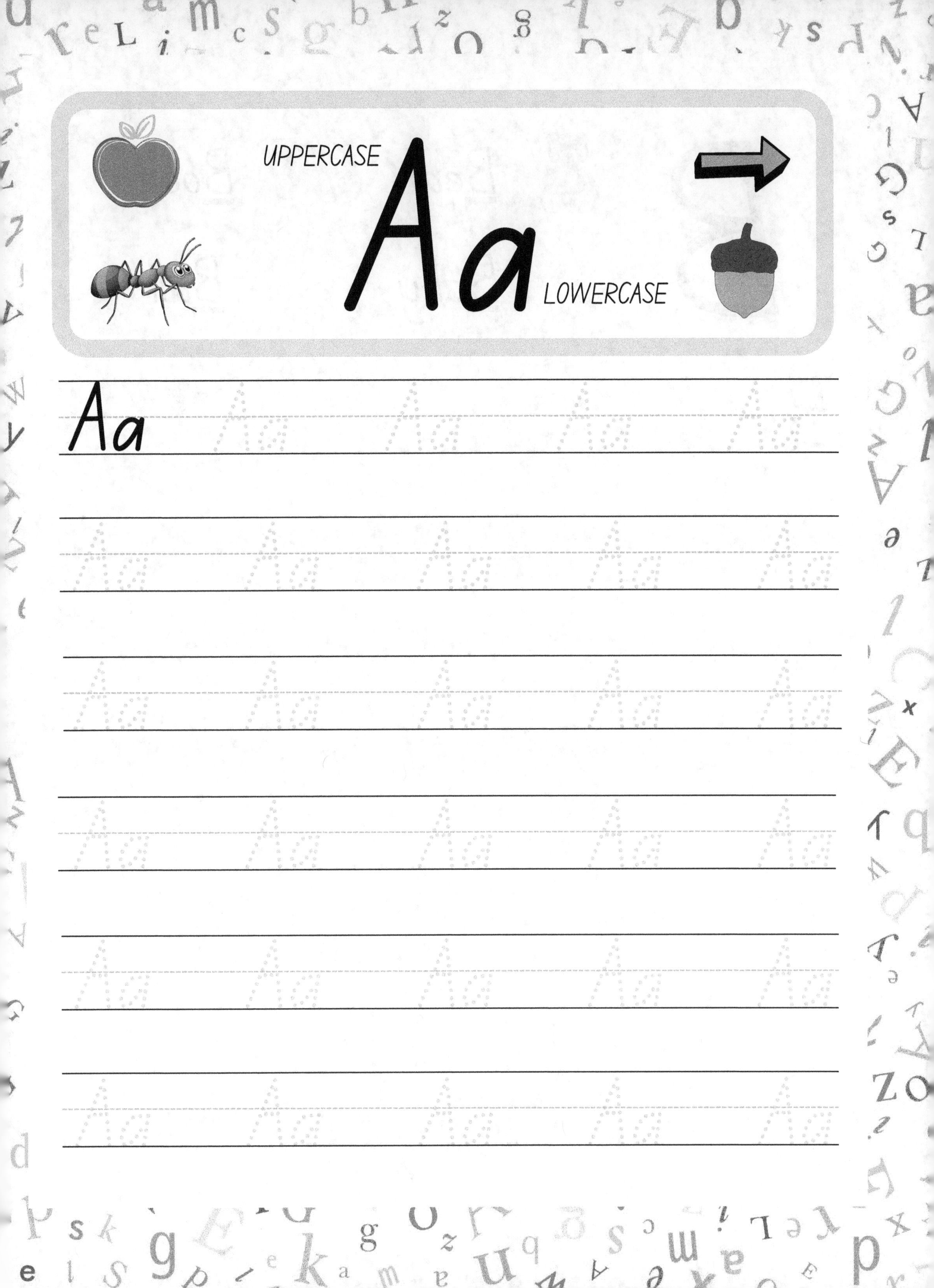
UPPERCASE
Aa
LOWERCASE
Aa

B

Bear

Book

Baby

Ball

B

b

bear

book

baby

ball

b

UPPERCASE
Bb
LOWERCASE
Bb

C

Candy Car

Cake Cup

C

c
candy
car
cake
cup
c

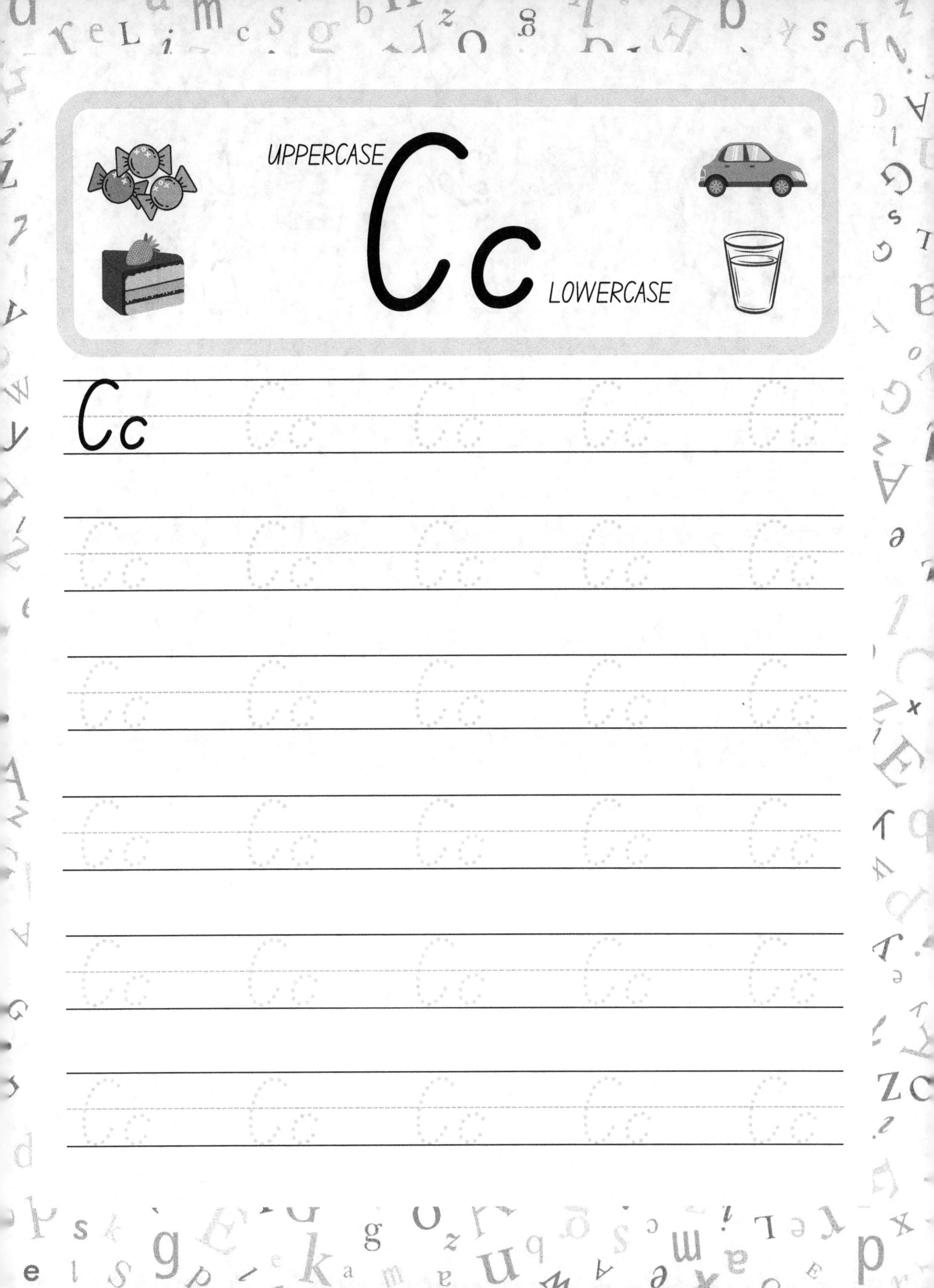
UPPERCASE
Cc
LOWERCASE
Cc

D

Dog

Door

Duck

Dime

D

d

dog

door

duck

dime

d

UPPERCASE Dd LOWERCASE

Dd

E

Egg

Ear

Elephant

Eagle

E

e

egg

ear

elephant

eagle

e

UPPERCASE **Ee** LOWERCASE

Ee

F

Fish

Fan

Frog

Fly

F

f

fish fan

frog fly

f

Ff

UPPERCASE

LOWERCASE

Ff

G

Grape

Goat

Ghost

Glove

G

g

grape

goat

ghost

glove

g

UPPERCASE
Gg
LOWERCASE
Gg

H

Heart

Hand

House

Hanger

H

h

heart hand

house hanger

h

UPPERCASE Hh LOWERCASE

Hh

I

Ice

Igloo

Insect

Iron

I

i

ice

igloo

insect

iron

i

UPPERCASE
Ii
LOWERCASE
Ii

J

Jet

Jar

Jacket

Jeans

J

j

jet

jar

jacket

jeans

j

UPPERCASE
Jj
LOWERCASE

K

Kite

King

Kitten

Knife

K

k

kite

king

kitten

knife

k

UPPERCASE
Kk
LOWERCASE
Kk

L

Lamp

Lizard

Ladybug

Ladder

L

l

lamp

lizard

ladybug

ladder

l

UPPERCASE
Ll
LOWERCASE
Ll

M

Monkey

Mirror

Mouse

Man

M

m
monkey
mirror
mouse
man
m

UPPERCASE
Mm
LOWERCASE
Mm

N

Nose

Nail

Necklace

Nest

N

n

nose

nail

necklace

nest

n

UPPERCASE
Nn
LOWERCASE
Nn

O

Orange

Oval

Octopus

Octagon

O

o

orange

oval

octopus

octagon

o

UPPERCASE
Oo
LOWERCASE
Oo

P

Pencil

Pipe

Paw

Pan

P

p

pencil

pipe

paw

pan

p

UPPERCASE

Pp

LOWERCASE

Pp

Q

Queen

Quilt

Quarter

“ ”

Quotes

Q

q

queen

quilt

quarter

" "

quotes

q

UPPERCASE

Qq

LOWERCASE

Qq

R

Rabbit Rainbow

Rope Rose

R

r
rabbit
rainbow
rope
rose
r

UPPERCASE
Rr
LOWERCASE
Rr

S

Snake

Spoon

Shoe

Spider

S

s

snake

spoon

shoe

spider

s

UPPERCASE
Ss
LOWERCASE
Ss

T

Turtle

Table

Tree

Thumb

T

t

turtle table

tree thumb

t

UPPERCASE
Tt
LOWERCASE
Tt

U
Umbrella
Up
Unicorn
Unicycle
U

u

umbrella

up

unicorn

unicycle

u

UPPERCASE
Uu
LOWERCASE
Uu

V

Violin

Vase

Vacuum

Volcano

V

V

violin

vase

vacuum

volcano

v

UPPERCASE

Vv

LOWERCASE

Vv

W

Water

Wave

Wood

Wig

W

w
water
wave
wood
wig
w

UPPERCASE
Ww
LOWERCASE
Ww

X
X-ray
Xylophone
X

X
x-ray
xylophone
x

UPPERCASE
Xx
LOWERCASE
Xx

y

Yarn

Yardstick

Yo-yo

Yacht

y

y

yarn

yardstick

yo-yo

yacht

y

UPPERCASE

Yy

LOWERCASE

Yy

Z

Zebra

Zero

Zipper

Zigzag

Z

Z

zebra

zero

zipper

zigzag

z

UPPERCASE
Zz
LOWERCASE
Zz

A-Z PRACTICE

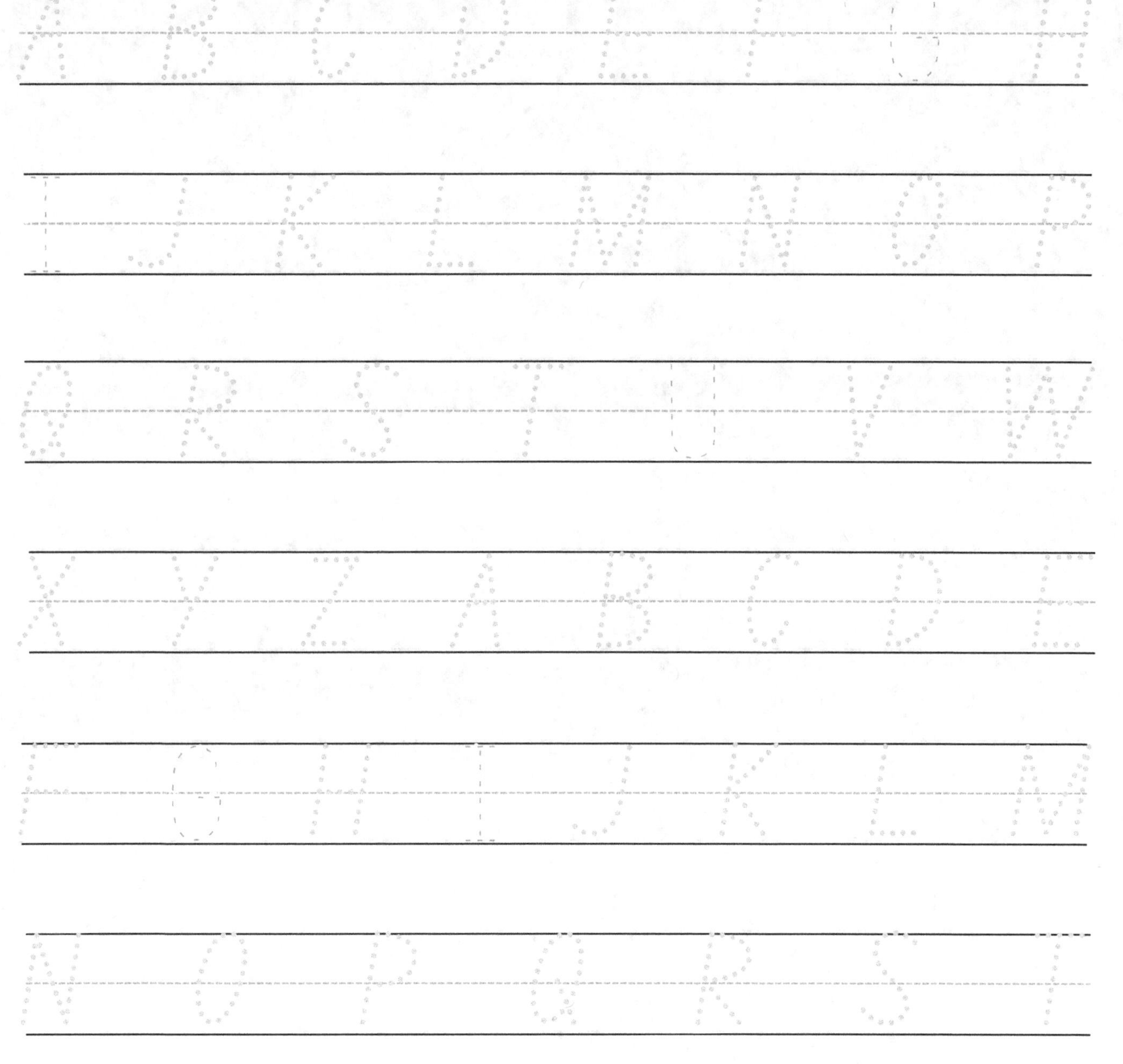

A-Z PRACTICE

A B C D E F G H

I J K L M N O P

Q R S T U V W

X Y Z A B C D E

F G H I J K L M

N O P Q R S T

U V W X Y Z

A-Z PRACTICE

A-Z PRACTICE

a-z PRACTICE

a b c d e f g h i j k l

m n o p q r s t u v w

x y z a b c d e f g h

i j k l m n o p q r s

t u v w x y z a b c d

e f g h i j k l m n o

p q r s t u v w x y z

a-z PRACTICE

a-z PRACTICE

a-z PRACTICE

FREE PRACTICE

FREE PRACTICE

FREE PRACTICE

FREE PRACTICE

FREE PRACTICE

FREE PRACTICE

FREE PRACTICE

FREE PRACTICE

FREE PRACTICE

FREE PRACTICE

FREE PRACTICE

FREE PRACTICE

www.ingramcontent.com/pod-product-compliance
Lightning Source LLC
Chambersburg PA
CBHW060516120726
48002CB00011B/3194
* 9 7 9 8 4 1 5 1 8 7 2 1 8 *